Sea Otter Pups

by Ruth Owen

Consultant:
Steve Shimek
Executive Director
The Otter Project
Monterey, California

BEARPORT
PUBLISHING

New York, New York

Credits

Cover and Title Page, © Donald M. Jones/Minden Pictures/FLPA; 4–5, © Donald M. Jones/ Minden Pictures/FLPA; 6–7, © Cusp/Superstock; 8, © Cosmographics; 9, © Suzi Eszterhas/ Minden Pictures/FLPA; 10–11, © Suzi Eszterhas/Minden Pictures/FLPA; 12–13, © Tom & Pat Leeson/Ardea.com; 14B, © Angel Simon/Shutterstock; 14–15, © Roberta Olenick/All Canada Photos/Superstock; 17T, © Tom & Pat Leeson/Ardea.com; 17B, © Suzi Eszterhas/ Minden Pictures/FLPA; 18–19, © Minden Pictures/Superstock; 20–21, © Kirsten Wahlquist/ Shutterstock; 22T, © NatalieJean/Shutterstock; 22C, © Donald M. Jones/Minden Pictures/ FLPA; 22B, © Ashley Whitworth/Shutterstock; 23T, © Maridav/Shutterstock; 23C, © S. Borisov/Shutterstock; 23B, © Katherine Welles/Shutterstock.

Publisher: Kenn Goin
Senior Editor: Lisa Wiseman
Creative Director: Spencer Brinker
Design: Emma Randall
Editor: Mark J Sachner
Photo Researcher: Ruby Tuesday Books Ltd

Library of Congress Cataloging-in-Publication Data

Owen, Ruth.
  Sea otter pups / by Ruth Owen.
    p. cm. — (Water babies)
  Includes bibliographical references and index.
  ISBN 978-1-61772-601-9 (library binding) — ISBN 1-61772-601-X (library binding)
  1. Sea otter—Infancy—Juvenile literature. I. Title.
  QL737.C25O94 2013
  599.769'5—dc23
                                    2012007274

For more information, write to Bearport Publishing Company, Inc., 45 West 21st Street, Suite 3B, New York, New York 10010. Printed in the United States of America.

10 9 8 7 6 5 4 3 2 1

Contents

Meet a sea otter pup

A mother sea otter and her **pup** are floating in the ocean.

The mother otter is resting on her back.

mother sea otter

The little pup is cuddled up on his mother's belly, just above the water.

sea otter pup

What is a sea otter?

Sea otters are animals that live in the ocean.

They are about as big as a medium-size dog.

Sea otters have very thick fur.

The fur helps keep the otter's body warm and dry in the cold water.

Adult sea otter size

thick fur

Where do sea otters live?

Although sea otters live in the ocean, they stay close to the **shore**.

The yellow parts of this map show where sea otters live.

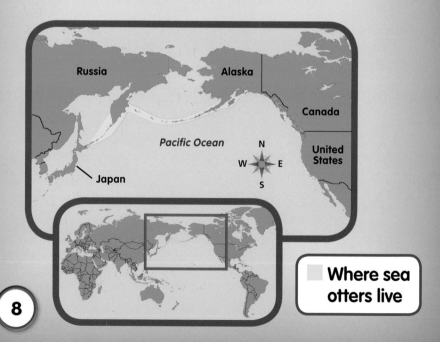

Russia

Alaska

Canada

Pacific Ocean

N
W   E
S

United States

Japan

Where sea otters live

shore

sea otters

A newborn pup

A mother sea otter gives birth in the ocean to just one pup at a time.

After the pup is born, she places it on her chest to keep it warm.

Then she feeds it milk from her body.

A pup drinks its mother's milk until it's about four to six months old.

mother sea otter

one-week-old pup

Learning to swim

A newborn sea otter cannot swim, but it can float really well.

It floats on top of the water like a beach ball!

floating pup

The mother sea otter gives her pup swimming lessons.

By the time it is about 14 weeks old, the pup is able to swim and dive.

floating mother sea otter

Sea otter food

Sea otter adults and pups eat crabs, clams, and other **shellfish**.

The mother otter dives under the water to hunt for food.

She teaches the pup how to dive and find shellfish, too.

clam

mother otter

crab

pup

Time for dinner

Once the mother sea otter finds a clam, she swims back up to the water's **surface**.

She also brings a rock with her and lays it on her belly.

Then she smashes the clam onto the rock to open its shell.

The mother otter and the pup share the clam meat.

clam

rock

clam
meat

sea otter
pup

mother
otter

Goodnight!

When it is time to sleep, an adult sea otter sometimes wraps **seaweed** around its body.

The seaweed, called **kelp**, is attached to the ocean floor.

It holds the otter in one place.

This keeps the waves from carrying the otter out into the ocean.

Sometimes the mother otter also wraps kelp around the pup as it sleeps on her chest.

sleeping adult
sea otter

kelp

Growing up

When a pup is between 6 and 12 months old, it leaves its mother.

It knows how to dive underwater to hunt for food.

It can use rocks to crack open shellfish.

The pup is now ready to begin its grown-up life!

clams

clam meat

Glossary

kelp (KELP) a type of seaweed that looks like long green or brown flat ribbons

pup (PUP) the baby of an animal such as a sea otter or a seal

seaweed (SEE-weed) living things that grow in oceans and look like plants

shellfish (SHEL-fish) sea creatures such as crabs and clams that live in water and have a hard outer shell

shore (SHOR) the land along the edge of an ocean, lake, or river

surface (SUR-fiss) the top layer of something, such as an ocean or river

Index

Read more

King, Zelda. *Sea Otters.* New York: PowerKids Press (2012).

León, Vicki. *A Raft of Sea Otters: The Playful Life of a Furry Survivor.* Montrose, CA: London Town Press (2005).

Ring, Susan. *Project Otter (Zoo Life).* Mankato, MN: Weigl (2003).

Learn more online

To learn more about sea otters, visit
www.bearportpublishing.com/WaterBabies

About the author

Ruth Owen has been writing children's books for more than ten years. She particularly enjoys working on books about animals and the natural world. Ruth lives in Cornwall, England, just minutes from the ocean. She loves gardening and caring for her family of llamas.